SCIENTIFIC
BREAKTHROUGHS

DISCOVERIES IN
LIFE SCIENCE

that changed the world

Rose Johnson

rosen publishing's
rosen
central®

Published in 2015 by The Rosen Publishing Group, Inc.
29 East 21st Street, New York, NY 10010

© 2015 Brown Bear Books Ltd

First Edition

Library of Congress Cataloging-in-Publication Data
Johnson, Rose, 1981- author.
 Discoveries in life science that changed the world / Rose
Johnson.
     pages cm. -- (Scientific breakthroughs)
Audience: Grades 5 to 8.
 Includes bibliographical references and index.
 ISBN 978-1-4777-8607-9 (library bound)
1. Life sciences--History--Juvenile literature. 2. Discoveries in
science--Juvenile literature. I. Title.
Q126.4.J64 2015
570.9--dc23

                          2014027233

Editor and Text: Rose Johnson
Editorial Director: Lindsey Lowe
Children's Publisher: Anne O'Daly
Design Manager: Keith Davis
Designers: Lynne Lennon
Picture Researcher: Clare Newman
Picture Manager: Sophie Mortimer

Brown Bear Books has made every attempt to
contact the copyright holder. If anyone has any
information please contact:
licensing@brownbearbooks.co.uk

All artwork: © Brown Bear Books

Manufactured in Malaysia

Contents

Introduction

Life science is the study of the most complicated things in the universe—living things. It investigates how life forms survive and where they came from.

As far as we know, Earth is the only planet to have life on it. This one planet has more than 8 million species of complex life, and perhaps millions more of simpler bugs and germs. An individual organism can be made up of trillions of cells all working together to keep the body alive. The human brain alone is thought to have more interconnections in it than there are stars in the Universe.

Being alive

Nevertheless, life scientists have discovered that all life works according to the same basic rules. To be alive, an object must be able to move, at least a little. It must have a source of energy to drive

The tiger is one of the biggest hunters on Earth and also one of the rarest.

Most of the life forms on Earth are trees and other plants. For every pound of animal on Earth, there are 1,000 pounds of plant.

its body processes. It must be able to respond to its surroundings, and above all it must be able to reproduce, to make a copy of itself.

Ecosystems

No organism lives by itself. There are always other life forms competing for food and other resources. Life science investigates how communities of organisms, or ecosystems, work. This knowledge is used to protect wildlife as it is threatened by human activities.

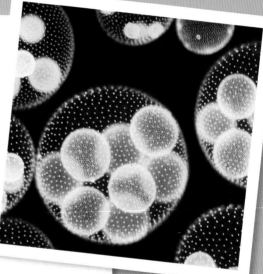

Natural history

Understanding how animals and plants live today also helps life scientists to figure out where they came from. It is thought that life has existed on Earth for 3.6 billion years, and 99 percent of the organisms that ever lived are now gone forever!

Many organisms are too small to see. Nearly 2,500 of these algae would just cover a dime.

5

Using Microscopes

The invention of the microscope revealed just how complex a living body is, and it showed that some organisms are too small to see with the naked eye.

The microscope was invented at the end of the 16th century, around the same time as the telescope. Both instruments work in a similar way, using a pair of lenses to magnify an image. Microscopes make a very small object appear much larger. One of the first people to look at living things through a microscope was the English scientist Robert Hooke (1635–1703).

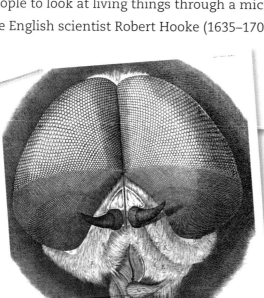

Robert Hooke used his microscope to investigate the intricate structure of living things such as the compound eye of a fly.

Microscopic world

Hooke made many drawings of the plant and animal features he saw. He published them in a book called *Micrographia* in 1665. Hooke's main discovery was that bodies were made of tiny units. He called them cells, after the little rooms that monks (and convicts) lived in.

A few years later the Dutch scientist Anton van Leeuwenhoek (1632–1723) used a microscope to discover what he called "animalcules"—microscopic, single-celled organisms such as bacteria and protists.

An electron microscope image of the underside of a sunflower leaf shows tiny spikes that make the leaf feel rough to the touch.

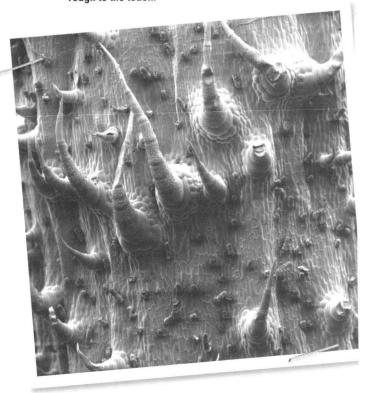

IMPLICATIONS

The first microscopes used light to make images. There is a limit to the size of object you can see with a light microscope, and many of the objects inside cells are too small to see. In the late 1920s, more powerful microscopes were invented. They used beams of particles called electrons, which could magnify things 100,000 times more than light. Electron microscopes have shown that cells are filled with even tinier structures called organelles.

Classifying Life

One of the main aims of life science is to organize living things into related groups. The system used today was devised in 1735 by Carl Linnaeus.

CARL LINNAEUS

Linnaeus was born in Sweden in 1707. He learned Latin before he could speak Swedish. Latin was the language of science in those days, and he used it as the language for his taxonomy system. Linnaeus published his taxonomy system in 1735 as the book *Systema Naturae* (meaning "nature's system"). Linnaeus then became a college professor. He died in 1778.

The field of life science that classifies organisms is called taxonomy. Linnaeus's taxonomy classified animals into groups according to how they looked.

Groups within groups

Linnaeus developed a hierarchy of groups that was able to show how closely related any two organisms were. The largest grouping was the "kingdom." All life was split between the animal kingdom and plant kingdom. (Fungi, bacteria, and other

These three life forms, the bird, mushroom, and moss all belong to separate kingdoms.

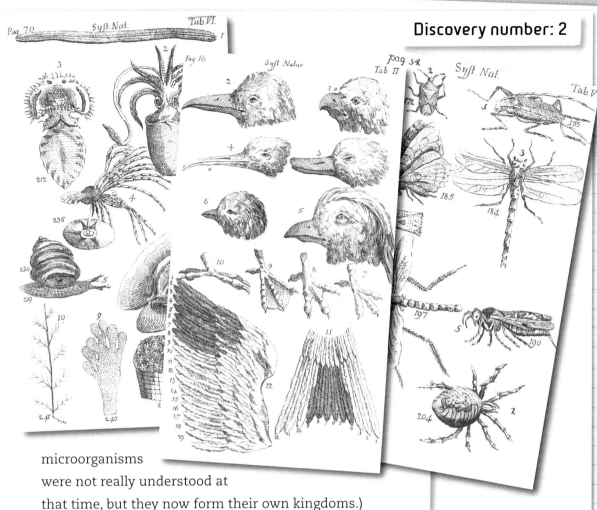

microorganisms
were not really understood at
that time, but they now form their own kingdoms.)

Smaller groups

The kingdoms were organized into classes. Animal classes included the mammals, birds, and insects. A class was subdivided into orders: Humans and monkeys were in the primate order, while lions and bears were in the carnivore order. Next came a family, followed by a genus, and finally every organism belonging to a species, the smallest grouping. Linnaeus gave every species two names. For example, a lion is *Panthera leo*. The first name was for the genus, (the general group of big cats), the second was the specific name for the lion species.

Linnaeus used these drawings of animal anatomy to show how each group of animals shared particular features.

9

Photosynthesis

Photosynthesis is the process used by plants to make the sugary food they need. This sugar is the main source of food for all animals as well.

Plants do not take in food, they make it themselves using photosynthesis. Biologists call organisms that survive like this autotrophs, which means "self eater." Some types of bacteria and other microscopic life forms are also autotrophs. Most of them use photosynthesis to make their food, while others use chemicals in rocks and water. Animals and fungi are heterotrophs ("other eaters"). They get their food by eating other organisms.

A green chemical in leaves, called chlorophyll, traps the energy from sunlight and uses it to make sugar.

1779, Jan Ingenhousz

Dutch biologist Jan Ingenhousz saw bubbles of oxygen coming from water plants in 1779. This was the first step in figuring out photosynthesis.

JAN INGENHOUSZ

Born in Breda in the Netherlands, Jan Ingenhousz qualified as a medical doctor. He had many other interests, such as the study of electricity, but he became famous for using vaccines to prevent the deadly disease smallpox. He became the doctor of the Austrian empress, and it was while living in Vienna that he made his discovery of photosynthesis.

Growth discovery

In the middle of the 17th century, a Belgian called Jan Baptist van Helmont (1580–1644) discovered that as a plant got larger, the mass of the soil it was growing in stayed more or less the same. That meant whatever was powering the plant's growth was coming from somewhere else. Van Helmont thought plants used water to grow, which explained why they wilted and died when the soil dried out.

Gas supply

In 1779, the Dutch researcher Jan Ingenhousz (1730–1799) discovered that during the day, a plant released oxygen gas. This is the opposite to what an animal does. Animals breathe in air and transfer some of its oxygen to their blood supply. The blood also releases carbon dioxide gas, which is then breathed out.

Cattle eat plants and get their energy from the sugars made by photosynthesis.

FACTS

- Chlorophyll uses the energy in blue and red light. Green light is reflected back, which is why plants look green.
- All the oxygen in Earth's atmosphere was put there by photosynthesis.
- Photosynthesis uses six times as much energy per day than the whole of human society.

The opposite of burning

The way that animals take in oxygen and give out carbon dioxide shows us that their body is burning food in a controlled way. When a food such as sugar is burned it reacts with oxygen to produce carbon dioxide and water—and it gives out energy. When this reaction takes place inside a body, it is called respiration. Respiration is the process that provides energy that powers all living bodies. However, if plants are giving out oxygen, and not carbon dioxide, then something else must be going on in plants that does not occur in other animals and other organisms.

Light and dark

In 1796 a Swiss priest, Jean Senebier (1742–1809) found that while plants were giving out oxygen, they were also taking in carbon dioxide. When the Sun went down, the plants started to give out carbon dioxide, just like animals do.

Making sugar

Photosynthesis is the opposite of respiration: Carbon dioxide and water react to make a sugar called glucose. Pure oxygen is a waste product, and is released from the plant. The sugar is the plant's fuel. Photosynthesis can only happen during daylight (the word means "making with light"). The energy that powers the reaction comes from sunlight. The light's energy is trapped by a green chemical in the leaves called chlorophyll.

Plants store their fuel as sugar. This is what makes fruits and other plants, such as this sugar cane, taste very sweet.

IMPLICATIONS

Food chains are a way of understanding how different living things get hold of the energy and nutrients they need. Photosynthesis is the first stage in every food chain. Plants are called producers—they produce the sugar that fuels the whole of life. Next come herbivores, which eat the plants. Carnivores eat the herbivores. (Omnivores eat a bit of both). Finally, detritivores eat the dead bodies, converting the nutrients back into soil.

Discovering Extinction

In 1813, it was shown that in the past the world was filled with different animals and other organisms that no longer survive.

Early fossil hunters had found the giant bones of what looked like elephants and rhinos in Europe and America. They thought that these were the same animals that now lived in Africa and Asia, but had been driven out by human hunters. They had also found fossils that did not match living species, such as giant bears and large lizards with wings. At the time most people believed

Millions of years ago the world was home to mammoths, woolly rhinos and saber-toothed tigers, all of which are now extinct.

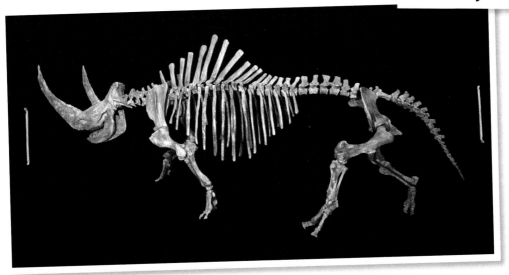

Rhinoceros fossils found in Europe are not the same species as the animals that live today in warmer parts of the world.

these were legendary monsters that had not been included on Noah's Ark during the Great Flood of Biblical times.

Long gone

In 1813, Frenchman Georges Cuvier (1769–1832) showed that fossil skeletons were different from those of living animals. He named the ancient elephants mastodons and also showed that a giant relative of the sloth, called megatherium, once lived in South America. He named the flying lizard "pterodactyl," now known to be a relative of dinosaurs. Cuvier had proved for the first time that it was possible for an animal to die out completely, or become extinct. About 45 years later Charles Darwin explained how new species evolved from old ones (see page 22).

IMPLICATIONS

The idea of extinction had a very large impact. Scientists who found fossils in deep rocks saw this as evidence that planet Earth was very old, many millions if not billions of years old. Extinctions seemed to happen throughout history, which suggested that it was a natural process. Perhaps an animal species died out because a new species took its place?

Chemistry of Life

An accidental discovery in 1828 revealed that the body's life processes work in the same way as any other chemical reactions.

Since ancient times, people thought that life relied on a vital force—a mysterious source of energy that made a body come alive. When an organism lost this vital force, it died. The physical body parts were still there, but they were as lifeless as a rock.

The white parts of bird dropping are rich in urea. Many other animals get rid of waste in the form of urea.

Spark of life

In the 1780s, Italian surgeon Luigi Galvani (1737–1798) thought he had discovered the vital force when he showed that electricity

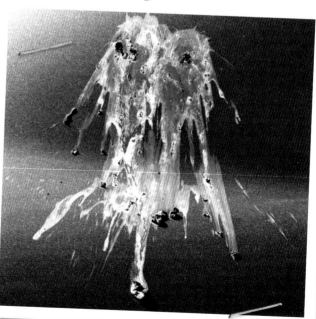

Bread dough rises because of bubbles of carbon dioxide that get trapped inside. The gas is produced by a biochemical reaction powered by yeast, tiny organisms mixed into the dough.

ran through bodies. However, this proved to be a mistake. In the end, it was a surprise discovery in 1828 that showed that a living body was powered by chemistry.

Surprising chemical

Friedrich Wöhler (1800–1882) was trying to make ammonium cyanate, which contains nitrogen, oxygen, and carbon atoms. Instead his experiment produced urea, which is a different chemical but made from the same ingredients. Until then it was thought that urea, which is the main component of urine, could only be made by a living body. Wöhler's breakthrough showed that the substances inside bodies followed the normal rules of chemistry. The modern field of biochemistry investigates the chemical processes that run inside bodies.

FACTS

- Chemicals that are made by living processes are described as organic. Sugars and fats are organic, as is petroleum oil.
- Most organic chemicals are made from the elements carbon, oxygen, hydrogen, nitrogen, calcium, and phosphorus.
- The main compounds in living bodies are proteins, fats, and carbohydrates, like sugar.

Cell Biology

Cells are the building blocks of a living body. They all share a set of characteristics but can perform many different roles.

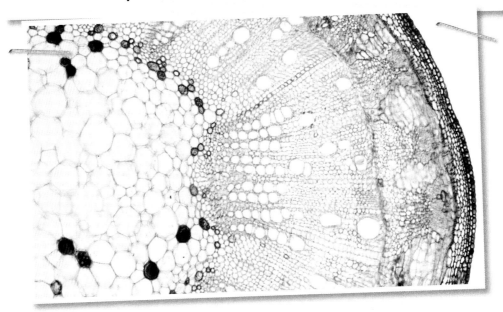

A slice of a plant stem shows that it is made from a collection of different cell types.

The cell was first described by Robert Hooke in the 1660s. Cells were seen inside all plants and animal bodies and even existed on their own as microorganisms. In 1838, Theodor Schwann, an expert on nerve cells, found that this type of cell, found only in animals, nevertheless shared many features with a plant cell. This link between such different organisms made him realize that cells are the most basic form of life. He developed a "cell theory," which states that all living organisms are composed of at least one cell, and every new cell arises from an older one.

What is a cell?

All cells are a bag of liquid called cytoplasm. Cytoplasm is water with chemicals like salts, proteins, and carbohydrates mixed into it. The cytoplasm is surrounded by a thin membrane. This is the outer edge of the cell. Membranes are made from layers of fat-like chemicals called lipids. Water can pass through the membrane, but most other substances cannot.

DNA store

All cells have genes in the form of DNA (see page 34). In bacteria cells, the DNA is in loose mass. In other cells the DNA is inside its own membrane, forming a structure called a nucleus. About 1,000 bacteria cells end to end would be as wide as the period at the end of this sentence. The cells of other organisms are about 100 times bigger.

THEODOR SCHWANN

Theodor Schwann was born in what is now Germany in 1810. He became an expert on the nervous system. One type of nerve cell is named for him. He set out his cell theory after discovering that all cells behaved in the same way—even those from completely different organisms. This led him to his cell theory in 1838. Schwann died in Germany in 1882.

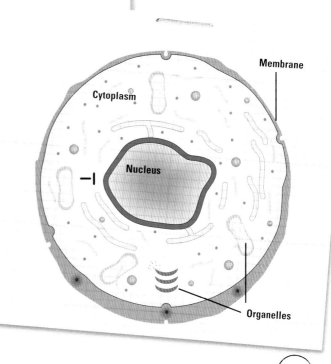

Cytoplasm

Membrane

Nucleus

Organelles

An animal cell has a flexible membrane around it. Inside is mainly a liquid called cytoplasm plus smaller structures called organelles.

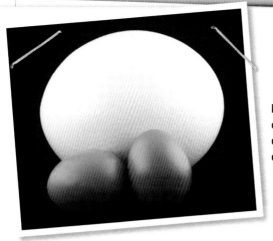

Bird eggs contain a single cell. The ostrich egg contains one of the largest cells in the animal kingdom.

Internal structures

By the 20th century, non-bacterial cells were found to have other structures called organelles, as well as a nucleus. Each organelle performs a particular job. A chloroplast in a plant cell is where photosynthesis takes place. The energy used by the cell is produced by the mitochondrion organelle. The endoplasmic reticulum is a system of tubes that makes and transports the substances the cell needs.

Single-cells

Single-celled organisms that have a body made from a complex cell are known as protists. They include things like amoebas, algae, and yeast. Protists have a varied lifestyle. Some eat food like an animal, others photosynthesize like a plant—some do both!

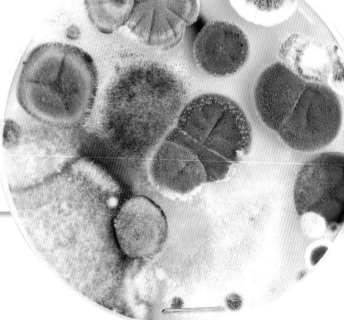

Molds are simple multi-celled fungi. The cells form long tubes that cover an object. It grows from a single cell called a spore.

FACTS

- The human body has about 100 trillion cells in it.
- Bacteria live in or on the human body (mostly in the digestive system). There are ten bacteria for every human cell in the body.
- A giant squid has nerve cells that are 39 feet (12 m) long.
- Some cells swim by wiggling a tail-like flagellum.
- Seaweeds are not really plants. Their cells are more closely related to protists called algae.

Red blood cells carry oxygen around the body. They are shaped a little like doughnuts to boost their surface area so they can absorb as much oxygen as possible.

Building a body

Plant, fungi, and animal bodies contain billions of cells working together. The cells resemble those of protists. Plant and fungi cells have stiff walls around the outside, while animal cells do not. The cells inside a body are not all the same. Cells specialize to perform a certain task. For example, blood cells are different to those in a bone or nerve. A group of specialized cells is called a tissue. A collection of tissues devoted to one aspect of the living body is called an organ.

Cell division

For a body to grow its cells must divide. The cell always divides in two. To do this the DNA needs to be copied into a second set so the "daughter" cells always have an identical set of genes as the parent cell.

Natural Selection

The theory of evolution by natural selection explains how living things can change over time.

Male stag beetles fighting. Natural selection was driven by competition between animals as they strove to survive and reproduce.

Charles Darwin's theory of evolution by natural selection is the most important breakthrough in life science. However, many people disagree with it because they believe it goes against religious teaching. Charles Darwin himself thought through his idea for many years before making it public. He was worried about its impact on religion. When another English scientist, Alfred Russell Wallace (1823-1913), outlined a similar idea to him, Darwin decided to explain his theory and wrote his famous book *On the Origin of Species* in 1859.

Many of Darwin's ideas came from observing animals that live on the Galápagos Islands in the Pacific Ocean. He saw that similar animals, like giant tortoises and birds, lived in different ways on each island.

Similarities and differences

As he traveled the world, Darwin saw that animals that were closely related lived in very different ways on different continents. Similarly, animals that were not related at all but lived in the same kinds of habitat around the world tended to look alike and live in similar ways.

Fight for survival

This gave Darwin the idea that species changed, or evolved, to suit their environment. The driving force for this evolution was competition for survival. In the natural world only the strongest, or "fittest" as Darwin called them, will survive. The process was very slow, but Darwin had learned from geologists, who study rocks, that Earth was very old indeed, and so there was time for evolution to happen.

CHARLES DARWIN

Charles Darwin was born in Shrewsbury, England, in 1809. While studying to be a priest in Oxford, he became interested in wildlife and decided to take a voyage around the world before joining the church. On his long trip, he had the idea of natural selection, and never took holy orders. He explained his idea in *On the Origin of Species* in 1859. Darwin died in 1882.

Frenchman Jean-Baptiste Lamarck (1744–1829) proposed another theory of evolution in 1809. He said that animal bodies change to suit their environment, like a blacksmith developed strong arm muscles. Their offspring would inherit these changes (blacksmith's sons had strong arms too). However, the inheritance system uncovered in 1863 showed that such a process was impossible.

According to Lamarck's theory, a giraffe's neck grows long because they keep stretching for the highest leaves.

Variation

A species is a group of animals that can breed with each other. Members of this group are very similar, but they are not identical. In a population of organisms all competing to get enough food and to find a mate, some individuals will be more successful. Their unique set of characteristics makes them fitter than others.

Survival of the fittest

The fittest individuals will have more offspring than their neighbors, who struggle to survive. This is known as natural selection—in the battle for survival, the fittest win. Parents pass on their unique characteristics to their offspring. Fit parents produce offspring with the same helpful characteristics. With each generation, those characteristics become more common in the population. The species has evolved into a slightly different animal than before. This process is called adaptation. Natural selection has produced animals that are well suited, or adapted, to the environmental conditions of the time. Over hundreds of millions of years, these tiny changes have all added up to make the many different types of life on Earth.

Random changes

If the environment changes, the characteristics that made individuals successful may no longer help. However, new characteristics are being introduced all the time by random changes in genes, called mutations. Most mutations are of no help, but occasionally one will boost an individual's fitness. In this way, natural selection is always at work.

Sharks are a type of fish, while dolphins are mammals. However, their bodies look very similar because natural selection has adapted them to a life swimming in the open ocean.

Inheritance

A monk experimenting with how pea plants grew led to the foundation of genetics. This field of life science is concerned with how parents pass on characteristics to their offspring.

GREGOR MENDEL

Born in 1822, Gregor Mendel worked as a gardener and beekeeper before becoming a monk and so had a good understanding of plant biology. His ideas about genes would become an important part of Darwin's theory of evolution. He began his work before Darwin published his ideas but did not release his own findings until 1863. Mendel died in 1884, and the importance of his work was not really properly understood until the 1900s.

In 1856 an Austrian monk called Gregor Mendel started to investigate why a crop of pea plants grew in such variety. He could see that pea plants were not all the same—they grew to different heights, had differently shaped pods, and developed flowers with different colors. In addition, the seeds from a plant with one set of characteristics grew into a new generation that were not always the same. His work led to the discovery of genes—although he died before his work became famous. It also took another 100 years before the chemical that carried genes, DNA, was fully understood.

Cross and recross

Over the next seven years he conducted a series of experiments that bred pea plants in a controlled way. He found that certain characteristics appeared more often than others. For example tall pea plants were more common than short ones. He described the tall characteristic as being dominant, and the short characteristic as being recessive. These terms are now applied to genes, although Mendel did not use the word *gene* himself.

Passing it on

Modern genetics, the science of genes and inheritance, talks about how parents pass on genes to offspring. Mendel's experiments revealed something about how organisms inherited characteristics. Pea plants can be crossed with themselves. That means that one plant can make seeds all by itself. (Many organisms need two parents to reproduce.) Mendel grew one plant that always produced tall offspring when crossed with itself. He also grew a plant that always produced short offspring. He then crossed these two and planted the seeds.

Mendel's experiments were looking at how seeds from one pea plant could produce plants that looked different from its parent.

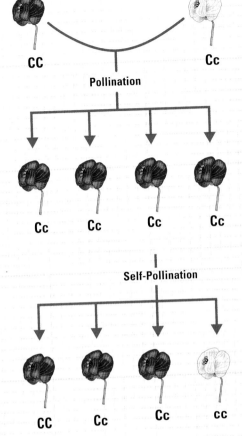

CC   Cc

Pollination

Cc   Cc   Cc   Cc

Self-Pollination

CC   Cc   Cc   cc

The C gene is dominant, making all the first generation of flowers solid pink. However, the recessive c gene is still there, so a quarter of all flowers in the second generation are striped.

Flower color was one of the factors investigated by Mendel. He found it was inherited in the same way as height.

Dominant and recessive

The offspring of the two plants were hybrids, meaning they had inherited a mix of characteristics from their parents. However, the first generation of hybrids were all tall. None were short. This meant that the tall gene was dominant and the short one was recessive. Whenever tall and short plants were hybridized the offspring would grow with the dominant characteristic.

Second generation

Then Mendel crossed one of the hybrids with itself. Three quarters of the second generation were tall, and a quarter were short. In other words the ratio of tall to short, was 3:1. Mendel showed that this ratio was always when the same when hybrids were crossed with themselves.

Alleles

We now understand that every pea plant has a double set of each gene. Each one in the pair is called an allele. The plants that Mendel began his experiment with had two alleles that were the same. The tall one was double dominant, the short one double recessive. The first generation of hybrids had one tall allele and one short, and so all grew tall. In the second generation three quarters had at least one dominant allele, while one quarter of them were double recessive.

Families look alike across the generations due to the way we inherit genes, as discovered by Gregor Mendel.

IMPLICATIONS

Later work on genetics found that not all genes could be described as dominant or recessive. Some are codominant, meaning they produce different characteristics when the alleles do not match to when they do. Nevertheless, Mendelian genetics can be seen working in all families. It is common for certain features to miss a generation, so children can share characteristics with their grandparents but not their parents.

Using Energy

All living bodies get the energy they need from a process called respiration. It is often described as "burning" food as fuel, but no flames are involved.

I t had been discovered in the 1780s that the human body—like all other animals—took in oxygen and gave out carbon dioxide. This indicated that the body was burning its food in some way, releasing energy and creating carbon dioxide and water. Carbon dioxide is toxic and so has to be released from the body as gas as we breathe out. The process that releases energy is called respiration. The primary source of energy is glucose, the simple sugar made by photosynthesis in plants.

The body of this runner is releasing energy from sugar as fast as possible so his muscles have the power to win the race.

MITOCHONDRIA

Respiration takes place in every cell of a living body. Cells contain many little structures called organelles. The organelles that handle respiration are called mitochondria. They are the power plants of the body. Cells that need to use a lot of energy, like muscles and nerves, contain large numbers of mitochondria.

Mitochondria are packed with folded membranes. The respiration process takes place on these surfaces.

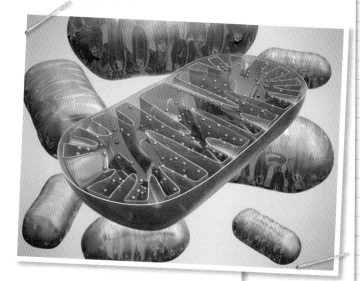

Chemical cycle

In 1937, the German scientist Hans Krebs (1900–1981) figured out how respiration worked. He found that each glucose molecule is rearranged 11 times into 11 different substances. At each step a little energy is released (instead of all of it in one go). The process is known as the citric acid cycle. The final molecule in the process is reused to help make the first molecule in the next cycle, which is citric acid.

Energy carrier

The energy released during respiration is stored by a molecule called adenosine triphosphate (ATP). Triphosphate means it has three phosphates on the molecule. When energy is needed, ATP breaks off one of the phosphates. That releases energy for powering muscles or another process. The ATP becomes ADP (adenosine diphosphate). The energy from each step of respiration is used to add a phosphate to these ADPs, making fresh ATP.

Primordial Soup

A lab experiment in 1953 showed that complex molecules used by living things could have arisen from simple chemicals in ancient oceans.

A lot of biology looks at how plants and animals live. The theory of evolution also looks at how they have changed over the long history of life on Earth. A big question remains. How did life begin? Before there was life, there was just a mixture of chemicals. This has been called the Primordial Soup (primordial means "in the beginning"). What process turned this soup of simple substances into the first living things?

Hot springs, like this one in Yellowstone National Park in Wyoming, are as close as we get to the Primordial Soup today.

Before life

Many of the chemicals we find in Earth's atmosphere and oceans come from living things. In the 1950s, the American astronomer Harold Urey (1893–1981) suggested that before there was life, Earth would have had the same kind of chemicals seen on other planets, such as carbon dioxide, methane, and ammonia.

Lollipop experiment

Urey's assistant Stanley Miller (1930–2007) suggested recreating the conditions of the ancient Earth. He put the chemicals suggested by Urey in a lollipop-shaped flask. He heated and cooled the mixture many times and sent electric sparks through it to create the effect of lightning. He let the process run for several days. Afterward he found that the simple chemicals had combined into more complex substances similar to the fats, sugars, proteins, and other chemicals that make up living things. This suggested that the first organisms could have formed from complex chemicals that had been cooked in the Primordial Soup for millions of years.

Stanley Miller watches his "lollipop" apparatus in action.

FACTS

- Earth is 4.6 billion years old. The first simple life forms, similar to bacteria, appeared about 3.6 billion years ago.
- Another theory suggests that the first simple life forms arrived frozen in the ice of a comet that hit Earth.
- The Primordial Soup was full of hydrogen sulfide and would have smelled like rotten eggs.

33

The Structure of DNA

DNA had been discovered in 1869, but it remained something of a mystery until its structure revealed how it could carry genetic code in 1953.

DNA is short for a much longer name: deoxyribonucleic acid. That name tells us that the compound contains a form of sugar called ribose. It is called a nucleic acid because it was soon associated with the nucleus of cells, where a similar chemical, RNA (ribonucleic acid) was also found.

James Watson (left) and Francis Crick show off a model of the DNA molecule.

Genetic material

By 1928 it was more or less certain that DNA was the substance that carried the genetic code as it was passed from parent to offspring, but no one knew how it did it.

Long molecule

Scientists knew that DNA was a polymer. This is a long molecule that is made up of smaller ones linked together in a chain. It was known that the chain in DNA was made up from ribose and four chemical "bases": adenine, thymine, cytosine, and guanine.

X-ray clue

In the early 1950s a technique using X-rays was used to investigate the shape of DNA. An X-ray photograph taken by English scientist Rosalind Franklin in 1952 gave the clearest view yet. Two scientists, American James Watson (1928–) and Englishman Francis Crick (1916–2004), used this photograph to figure out that DNA was a double helix, or a spiral with two strands.

Putting it all together

The double helix is like a twisted ladder. The two sides of the "ladder" are made from chains of ribose molecules, which are held together by phosphates, linkages made from phosphorus and oxygen. Pairs of bases run between the two ribose chains, forming the "rungs" of the ladder.

Rosalind Franklin's X-ray photo played an essential role in figuring out the structure of DNA

ROSALIND FRANKLIN

Born in London, England, in 1920, Franklin worked as a scientist for her whole adult life. She was an expert in coal, but changed to X-ray diffraction, a technique for making images of complex molecules. She used it to produce Photo-51, which helped unlock the secrets of DNA. However, her contribution to the discovery was not recognized until long after she had died of cancer in 1958.

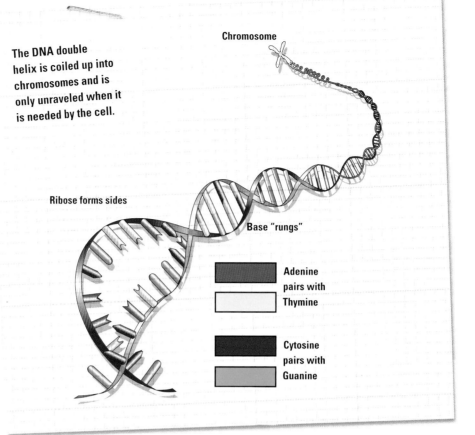

The DNA double helix is coiled up into chromosomes and is only unraveled when it is needed by the cell.

Chromosome

Ribose forms sides

Base "rungs"

Adenine pairs with Thymine

Cytosine pairs with Guanine

Code carrier

The four bases form pairs. Guanine always bonds to cytosine, while adenine bonds to thymine. These four units form a four-letter code that runs along the DNA molecule. Scientists use the letters A, G, C, and T to keep things simple. A human cell has 46 strands of DNA that contain the code for 20,000 genes made up from 2 billion bases. The DNA molecule is very long and thin—the length of all the DNA from a single human cell is about 6.5 feet (2 m).

Reading the code

Each gene is spelled out in the four-letter code along one side of the DNA molecule. The opposite pair for each base fits on top to complete the polymer. To function, the cell needs to read the DNA.

Everyone has a blood group gene, either A, B, AB, or O. This is the code for the proteins that grow on the outside of red blood cells.

To do that, the double helix is unzipped, dividing it into two strands, revealing the one that carries the code. Every gene is an instruction manual for making a particular protein.

Making proteins

Proteins are polymers as well. They are made up of hundreds of smaller units called amino acids. The natural world uses around 20 amino acids to make all proteins. The precise order of the different acids gives each protein a unique shape, and that shape helps it perform its job inside the cell. Every three base letters on the DNA stands for a particular amino acid. After the DNA has been unzipped, a copy is made using the other nucleic acid RNA. This travels to an organelle outside the nucleus called a ribosome, where its code is translated and used to construct the proteins the body needs.

Every person's DNA is unique. A DNA fingerprint converts the different genes a person has into a pattern that can be used to identify them.

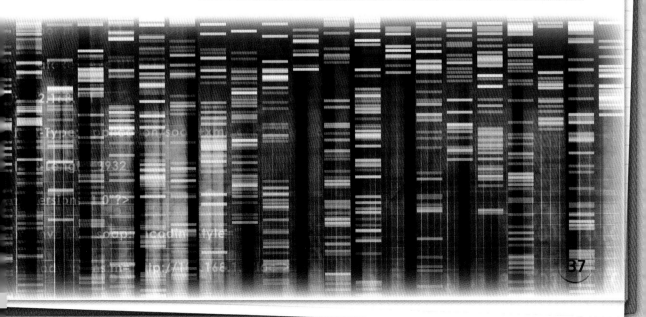

Genetic Engineering

Learning how the genetic inheritance system worked allowed scientists to figure out ways to control it and make new types of organisms.

Genetic engineering is a technology that allows scientists to alter the genes in an organism. It has been used to make medicines and drought-resistant crops, and it may help cure inherited diseases.

Adding DNA

Genetic engineering began in the 1970s. The first genetically engineered animal was created

Genetic engineering takes place in laboratories where DNA is made in large amounts and then added to the cells of plants and animals.

FACTS

- Crops have been genetically engineered to withstand frost and attacks by fungus.
- In the future, genetic engineering might cure inherited diseases.

This mouse has had jellyfish genes added to it that make it glow in the dark.

in 1974 by the German scientist Rudolf Jaenisch (b.1942). He produced a mouse that had the genes from a bacteria added to it.

Useful virus

A body begins as a single cell called a zygote, which then divides into billions more. Genetic engineers must insert a gene into the zygote, so the whole body can make use of it. The most common method is to add a gene using a virus. Natural viruses add genes to the DNA in a cell. Genetic engineers make artificial viruses to introduce the desired gene.

Concerns

Many people have concerns about genetic engineers altering natural life forms. Researchers get permission to do their experiments and must ensure that the new varieties of organism they create are safe.

BREEDING

People have been controlling the genes in animals for centuries. Plants and animals have been transformed into new forms (with particular genes) by artificial breeding. Two parents that have good characteristics—they grow sweet fruits or have very woolly coats—are made to breed. Their offspring will have the same characteristics too. Over many generations this process can transform a natural organism into many different breeds.

Black Smokers

On the deep seabed, unusual ecosystems live around hot plumes of volcanic water. It is the only wildlife community that can survive without the Sun's energy.

It used to be thought that all life on Earth was powered by energy from the Sun. Plants use sunlight to make food, and then animals eat the plants (or each other).

Hydrothermal vent

In 1977 a team led by Jack Corliss discovered hydrothermal vents at the bottom of the Pacific Ocean. These were jets of hot water that flooded out of cracks in the seabed. The water

Deep-sea submersibles were used to find hydrothermal vents.

was heated by volcanic activity deep beneath the seabed and was full of chemicals, such as hydrogen sulfide. This makes the water look like smoke, so the vents are called "black smokers."

Vent life

No plants can grow in the darkness on the seabed. However, bacteria survive around the hot vents using hydrogen sulfide as a source of energy. The bacteria are eaten by larger animals, such as mussels, clams, and giant tube worms. These ecosystems, or wildlife communities, are able to survive without sunlight.

Tiny crabs prey on the mussels that live on the seabed around black smokers.

IMPLICATIONS

The conditions around black smokers are extreme compared to the rest of Earth. However, they are also constant—they don't change. It has been suggested that the first life forms evolved in environments like this, while the rest of the young planet was being blasted frequently by meteorites and frozen in ice ages.

The water close to the vent is hot enough to kill most life forms. Only bacteria can survive these extreme conditions.

41

Death of the Dinosaurs

The best explanation for the sudden disappearance of dinosaurs 66 million years ago proposes that a huge meteor hit Earth and wiped them out.

The meteor thought to have killed the dinosaurs was about the size of Manhattan Island. It hit Mexico at an angle and sent a fireball across North America.

A fossil is a snapshot of life at a particular moment in the long history of Earth. Scientists can figure out how old a fossil is by the age of the rocks it is found in.

Age of dinosaurs

The oldest dinosaur fossils are found in rocks around 220 million years old. Many more are found in younger rocks. But 66 million years ago, dinosaur fossils disappeared completely. This indicates that the dinosaurs all became extinct at the same time.

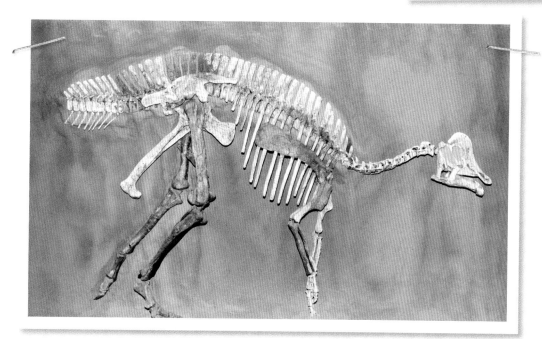

Out with a bang

In 1980 a father and son, Luis (1911–1988) and Walter Alvarez (1940–), proposed that the dinosaurs had become extinct after Earth was hit by a giant meteor. The American scientists had found a thin layer of dust in rocks all over the world, which showed that the impact had created a cloud so huge it enveloped the planet.

Harsh environment

The meteor, which hit in what is now Mexico, would have caused huge fires and tsunamis that devastated much of the land. The cloud of dust blocked out the Sun for years, killing plants. Without enough food, large animals like dinosaurs died out very quickly.

Everything we know about dinosaurs comes from their fossilized skeletons.

IMPLICATIONS

The death of the dinosaurs was part of a mass extinction. Three-quarters of all life on Earth died at the same time. There have been four other mass extinctions in the history of Earth. Why they happen is still a mystery. As well as meteor strikes, they could be caused by huge volcanic eruptions or rapid climate changes.

Cloning

A clone is an organism that contains exactly the same set of genes as another. In the 1990s scientists figured out how to make cloned animals.

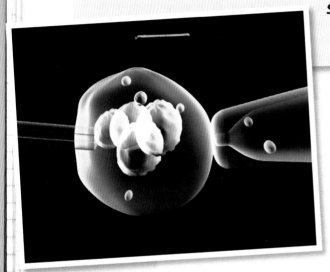

Cloning technology transfers the nucleus of one cell into another using a microscopic needle.

Most large animals, such as mammals, birds and reptiles, reproduce sexually. That means every individual is produced by two parents, one of which is male and the other female. Other organisms are able to reproduce asexually. That is, one parent makes exact copies, or clones, of themselves. Cloning technology copies this second system.

Half set of genes

For sexual reproduction, a parent produces sex cells. Males make sperm, females make eggs. Each sex cell has only a half set of DNA. When an egg and sperm join together in a process called fertilization, the half sets combine to make a brand new full set of DNA. This set is unique to that new individual.

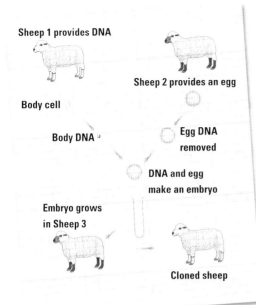

Sheep 1 provides DNA

Sheep 2 provides an egg

Body cell

Body DNA

Egg DNA removed

DNA and egg make an embryo

Embryo grows in Sheep 3

Cloned sheep

Three female sheep are involved in producing one cloned sheep.

Moving DNA

In 1996, the first mammal clone, a sheep called Dolly, was produced in Scotland by a team led by Keith Campbell (1954–2012). The scientists took an egg cell from one sheep and removed its half set of DNA. They then replaced it with a full set of DNA taken from a body cell of another sheep (the one being cloned). This process turned the egg into an embryo, which developed into Dolly. Dolly lived for just six years, half the normal age of a sheep. This might indicate that DNA has a natural timer built in. When Dolly was born, her DNA was still set at the same age as the older sheep from which it was originally taken.

IMPLICATIONS

Cloning humans is prohibited, but identical twins are naturally genetically identical. Twins help researchers to study how much of a person's characteristics, such as personality and intelligence, are controlled by their genetic code and how much of it is from the environment they grew up in.

Identical twins are natural clones of one another.

45

TIMELINE

1665: Robert Hooke looks at the plants and animals through a microscope for the first time. He is the first person to record—and name—cells.

1735: Carl Linnaeus develops the system for organizing the living world into groups of related organisms.

1779: Jan Ingenhousz discovers that plants release oxygen when exposed to sunlight. This is the first evidence of photosynthesis.

1812: Georges Cuvier proves that the animals that lived in the past are now extinct.

1828: Friedrich Wöhler discovers that the chemicals made by living things can also be made in laboratories.

1838: Cell theory, which states that cells are the basic units of living things, is developed.

1859: Charles Darwin publishes his theory of evolution by natural selection.

1863: Gregor Mendel discovers genetics by investigating how characteristics are inherited.

1938: Hans Krebs figures out the process by which respiration releases energy from sugar.

1953: Stanley Miller highlights how the Primordial Soup might have been able to generate life from nonliving chemicals.

1953: The structure of DNA is revealed, showing how the chemical can store coded instructions.

1974: Genetic engineers succeed in creating the first animal with genes from an unrelated organism.

1977: A new form of life, that gets its energy from chemicals, is discovered living around hot springs on the seabed.

1980: A new theory proposes that dinosaurs were wiped out by a giant meteor hitting Earth.

1996: Dolly the sheep becomes the first mammal clone.

GLOSSARY

amino acid: The building blocks of a protein.

carbohydrate: A substance made from carbon, oxygen, and hydrogen. Simple ones are sugars. Sugars chained together make complex carbohydrate, like starch.

cell: The smallest unit of a living body.

energy: The ability to change the structure of chemicals, which is the basis of all life processes, from movement to digestion.

fossil: The remains of a dead plant or animal that has been preserved in rock.

glucose: A simple sugar made by photosynthesis.

membrane: A thin and flexible barrier. All cells are surrounded by a membrane.

nucleic acid: A chemical that carries the genetic code. DNA is the main nucleic acid.

organelle: A structure within a cell that carries out life processes.

phosphate: A substance that contains phosphorus and oxygen. Phosphates are common in the complex chemicals of a living body.

protein: A substance used in all living things. Proteins are used in muscles and skin, and as enzymes.

zygote: The first cell of a body.

FOR MORE INFORMATION

BOOKS

Landon, Melissa (ed.). *Biology: Understanding Living Matter*. New York: Britannica Educational Publishing, 2015.

Murphy , Glenn. *Evolution: The Whole Life on Earth Story*. London: Pan Macmillan, 2014.

Spilsbury, Louise. *Survival of the Fittest: Extreme Adaptations*. New York: Gareth Stevens Publishing, 2015.

WEB SITES

Because of the changing nature of Internet links, Rosen Publishing has developed an online list of websites related to the subject of this book. This site is updated regularly. Please use this link to access this list:

http://www.rosenlinks.com/SCIB/Life

INDEX